21ST
Century
Skills Library

REAL WORLD MATH: NATURAL DISASTERS

WILDFIRES

BY TAMRA B. ORR

CHERRY
LAKE
Publishing

Published in the United States of America by
Cherry Lake Publishing, Ann Arbor, Michigan
www.cherrylakepublishing.com

Content Adviser
Jack Williams, Founding Editor of the *USA Today* weather page and author of *The
AMS Weather Book: The Ultimate Guide to America's Weather*

Math Adviser
Katherine M. Gregory, M.Ed

Credits
Cover and page 1, ©Neale Cousland/Shutterstock, Inc.; page 4, ©AP Photo/Mike
Meadows; page 6, ©AP Photo/Gus Ruelas; page 8, ©OlegD/Shutterstock, Inc.;
page 10, ©alsamua/Shutterstock, Inc.; page 14, ©Chris Pole/Shutterstock,
Inc.; page 16, ©Samuel Acosta/Shutterstock, Inc.; page 19, ©John Brueske/
Shutterstock, Inc.; page 20, ©My Portfolio/Shutterstock, Inc.; page 22,
©Portokalis/Shutterstock.com; page 24, ©TFoxFoto/Shutterstock.com; page 26,
©Brian Weed/Shutterstock, Inc.

Library of Congress Cataloging-in-Publication Data
Orr, Tamra.
 Wildfires/by Tamra B. Orr.
     p. cm.—(Real world math)
 Includes bibliographical references and index.
 ISBN 978-1-61080-329-8 (lib. bdg.)—ISBN 978-1-61080-338-0 (e-book)—
ISBN 978-1-61080-412-7 (pbk.)
 1. Wildfires—Juvenile literature. 2. Mathematics—Juvenile literature. I. Title.
II. Series.
 SD421.23.O77 2012
 363.37'9—dc23   2011033562

Cherry Lake Publishing would like to acknowledge
the work of The Partnership for 21st Century Skills.
Please visit *www.21stcenturyskills.org* for more information.

Printed in the United States of America
Corporate Graphics Inc.
January 2012
CLSP10

TABLE OF CONTENTS

CHAPTER ONE
EATING UP THE ACRES

Agua Dulce, a community near Los Angeles, California, was hotter than usual in October 2007. There were no cool breezes blowing through to bring relief to people. No autumn rains had wet the ground. The dry Santa Ana winds

Firefighters worked hard to put out the flames in Agua Dulce.

were blowing, making the ongoing **drought** seem even hotter and drier. A young boy, bored and with nothing to do, grabbed a box of matches from his home and went outside.

Minutes later, the harmless game he thought he was playing with the matches turned into the Buckweed Fire. One small flame quickly ate up the dry grass and eagerly searched for something else to devour. The fire grew and spread wildly. By the time it finally ended several days later, more than 38,000 acres (15,378 hectares) had been scorched. Twenty-one houses were destroyed. Five people were injured, and 15,000 people had to be evacuated from their homes.

LEARNING & INNOVATION SKILLS

Firefighters who have found themselves trapped in a blazing forest know the value of a good fire shelter. The shelters are tents made of aluminum, which can reflect intense heat and keep a firefighter protected inside. The newest type of fire shelter is one that closes automatically when it senses heat approaching. It also blocks flying **embers** from entering the structure. Special vents allow the firefighters inside to breathe until the fire passes.

Before the fall season was over, more than three dozen fires had raced through the region. The **wildfires** burned more than 500,000 acres (202,343 ha) and destroyed about 1,600 houses. Adding to the disaster were **arsonists**, who took pleasure from starting additional fires. California governor Arnold Schwarzenegger advised the arsonists to turn themselves in to police. "If I were one of the people who started the fires, I would not sleep soundly right now, because we're right behind you," he warned.

The 2007 wildfires caused serious destruction throughout California.

REAL WORLD MATH CHALLENGE

The chart below shows the number of fires and the number of acres they destroyed in the United States from 2000 to 2010. What is the total number of fires that occurred? In what year were the most acres destroyed? The fewest? What is the difference in acres destroyed between these two years?

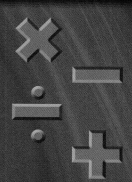

Year	Number of Fires	Number of Acres Destroyed
2000	92,250	7,393,493
2001	84,079	3,570,911
2002	73,457	7,184,712
2003	63,629	3,960,842
2004	65,461	8,097,880
2005	66,753	8,689,389
2006	96,385	9,873,745
2007	85,705	9,328,045
2008	78,979	5,292,468
2009	78,792	5,921,786
2010	71,839	3,422,823

(Turn to page 29 for the answers)

Every year, thousands of wildfires rage across the United States. News programs show images of exhausted firefighters, ruined homes, scorched forests, and crackling flames. Given their destructive powers, it's easy to think of a wildfire as an enemy or a monster. But since the beginning of time, forest fires have been a normal and helpful part of nature's cycle.

Fires are nature's way of removing dead branches, bushes, and grasses, and preparing land for new growth. In many ecosystems, they help keep growth under control and help maintain healthy conditions. In the past, many fires burned

Forest fires are not always harmful.

out before they did any serious damage. But that is not true today.

With each passing year, the number of fires around the world seems to grow. Rich Ochoa, of the National Interagency Fire Center, says, "We are seeing a significant trend. Over the last 10, 12 years, fire activity has been much higher than normal."

Why is this true? Experts offer different reasons. Many blame it on how well firefighters have been able to control fires. Snuffing out small fires quickly has actually allowed forests to become overgrown with old needles, leaves, and branches. When these build up on the forest floor, they create perfect **tinder** for a fire. Other experts suggest that fire activity has increased because of the large number of homes and businesses built in and around forests. Those structures provide more tinder for the flames.

A number of experts also point to global warming as a cause of heightened fire activity. Many researchers claim global warming is responsible for higher temperatures in certain regions. Some believe it might also be the cause of the increasing number of droughts. Additionally, with higher temperatures, winter snows occur later than usual and existing snow melts earlier. This leaves the land drier for longer periods of time.

Whatever the cause, wildfires are a huge problem throughout the world—one that is not likely to improve in coming years.

CHAPTER TWO
A DANGEROUS TRIANGLE

Fires of any kind can only start if they have three ingredients: oxygen, fuel, and heat. These three ingredients are often called the fire triangle. All three must be present for fire to occur. As soon as one burns up, runs out, or dies out, the fire will end.

Dead trees and branches can provide fuel for forest fires.

Oxygen is always present in the forest, where many fires originate. In the forest, fuel can be branches, logs, grass, leaves, and bushes. Items such as paper, wooden fences, outbuildings, and houses can also fuel fires. Other types of fuel include coal, gasoline, and oil. Gases such as propane, butane, and natural gas can also serve as fuel in the fire triangle.

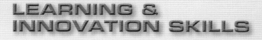

LEARNING & INNOVATION SKILLS

Over the years, the technology used to fight fires has become more effective. Foams and powders that **extinguish**, or put out, fires as fast as or faster than water have been developed. According to a group of researchers at Harvard University in Massachusetts, someday firefighters will fight flames with blasts of electric current. Researchers have found that if an electrical charge is powerful enough, it can change the shape of flames and even put them out completely. An electric blaster would allow firefighters to create a safe path into a burning building or open up a rescue route for people trapped inside.

The third ingredient, heat, is the one that turns oxygen and fuel into fire. But in the wilderness, where does this heat come from? Sometimes lightning striking the ground provides the heat. Power lines torn down by high winds can provide heat from the electricity running through them. In some regions, lava or hot ash from volcanic activity can provide the heat to ignite a fire.

A fire often starts from natural causes. But by far, the main cause of wildfires is human activity. When Smokey Bear says, "Only *you* can prevent forest fires," he's being quite honest. People cause four of out every five wildfires. Arsonists deliberately set some of these fires. Arson is the leading cause of fires in the United States—and statistics show that young people start many of them. One-half of those arrested for arson are under the age of 18.

Many fires are caused by humans who were not trying to start one. These people would be horrified to learn that they were responsible for causing a fire. This includes the person who tosses a burning cigarette out the car window. It includes the camper who leaves the campsite without making sure that the campfire is completely out. The youngster setting off fireworks on the Fourth of July would be shocked to learn that he or she started a fire. So would someone playing in a field with a pack of matches. The same is true of an unlucky person whose house burns down and then starts a fire in the neighborhood.

Even small human actions can set into motion a huge fire that can destroy entire forests and communities. As Smokey Bear advises, it's essential that everyone take precautions to

REAL WORLD MATH CHALLENGE

The following chart shows the number of fires started by different causes. Look at the chart and answer the questions below.

Number of Fires (per 100)	Cause of Fires
44	Arson
22	Children playing/accidents
11	Smoking/lighters/matches
8	Campfires
6	Burning debris, leaves, etc.
6	Equipment failure
3	Lightning strikes

a. What causes fires twice as often as lightning strikes?
b. What causes fires half as often as children playing/accidents?
c. What causes fires four times more than smoking/lighters/matches?

(Turn to page 29 for the answers)

prevent forest fires. We may not be able to stop volcanoes from erupting or bolts of lightning from striking the earth. But we can put out fires and handle any flame or burning object with extreme caution.

CHAPTER THREE

DO THE MATH: FROM GROUND TO CROWN

If you watch coverage of wildfires on television news reports, you may think all fires are alike. Each seems to have

Sometimes dry grass and the right weather conditions are all it takes to start a fire.

red-orange flames that dance with the wind as they consume whatever is in their path. Firefighters, however, know that each fire is unique. These professionals know that there are many different kinds of fires, depending on where the blaze is occurring.

Some fires start on the forest floor, among the dry leaves and rotted pieces of wood. These are called ground fires. They usually spread slowly because they do not have a lot of access to oxygen. Even so, they produce quite a lot of smoke. In some forests, they can smolder and burn for weeks or months.

Surface fires burn on the forest's surface, meaning the grass, the trees, and the bushes. They spread very quickly and produce a great deal of flames. These fires rarely burn all the way to the forest floor.

The most dangerous types of fires are those that are fueled by winds and rush straight to the upper part of the tree. Called crown fires, their flames leap from treetop to treetop. They often turn into **firestorms**, powerful blazes that actually create their own wind systems. Crown fires usually use ladder fuels to reach the canopy of the forest. Ladder fuels are shrubs, fallen trees, and branches that burn quickly and lead the flames up higher. These fires commonly consume all trees and shrubs in their path.

Spot fires are those created by **firebrands**, or the embers of a fire, that have been tossed by the wind to a different location. Often they burn long enough to merge with other fires to create a huge wall of flames. These are often almost impossible for firefighters to get under control.

Depending on its type, a wildfire can travel 2 to 3 miles (3.2 to 4.8 kilometers) per hour in thick, dense forests. It can travel up to 14 miles (22.5 km) per hour over open grasslands. A strong wind can move the flames faster over the terrain, helping them reach speeds of up to 60 miles per hour (96.6 kph). Southern California's Santa Ana winds, for example, blow from the east-northeast during the fall and winter. These hot, dry winds tend to make fires even more deadly.

Some wildfires create thick, black smoke clouds.

In 1911, a forester named William B. Osborne Jr. grew concerned about the likelihood of devastating fires in the Oregon forests. When he was not busy working for the state's Forest Services, he was in his workshop at home, tinkering with a special invention. Osborne called his invention a firefinder. The device was a map of the forest mounted on a rotating steel disc. It included sighting instruments made from brass. Osborne's invention made it possible to accurately pinpoint the location of a forest fire by tracking its smoke.

By 1913, firefinders were being used in forests all over the country. Over the years, Osborne continued to improve his creation. He added more powerful sighting scopes and more

REAL WORLD MATH CHALLENGE

2011 was a destructive year in the southwestern United States. Between January 1 and October 31, nearly 26,000 fires were reported across Texas. Thanks to accurate fire reports and fast response from firefighters, almost 37,000 homes were saved.

On average, how many new fires began each day? How many homes were saved each day? Round your answers to the nearest whole number.

(Turn to page 29 for the answers)

precise formulas for calculating distances. One century later, firefinders are still being used.

Osborne was also influential in helping to establish lookout towers in many of the nation's forests. These very tall towers are manned by people who watch all summer long for the first sign of smoke. They also record how many lightning strikes hit the ground. These workers put in very long hours and are often alone. Most towers survey about 1,500 square miles (3,885 square km). These towers are more commonly found in the western parts of the United States.

LIFE & CAREER SKILLS

Does hanging over the edge of an airplane with a parachute strapped to your back sound exciting? If so, you might consider a job as a **smokejumper**. But before you make that decision, remember that thick smoke and crackling flames are waiting for you below! Professional firefighters often have 10 to 20 years of experience before they become smokejumpers. Many of them also have degrees in fire management, forestry, or engineering. You must be in tip-top physical shape. You also must take a difficult 5-week course that teaches parachuting and other special skills to become a smokejumper. Of course, bravery is a good skill to bring along, too!

Towers are built up high, where a lookout has a wide view of the surrounding forest.

When someone in the lookout tower spots smoke, he or she radios a report to a special dispatcher. The precise location of the smoke is reported. Descriptions of its color and shape are given. The direction and speed it is moving is also reported. White smoke typically means a grass fire. Dark blue or black smoke often means that trees are on fire. The dispatcher relays this vital information to firefighters. That way, the firefighters will head in the right direction with the proper equipment.

CHAPTER FOUR
DO THE MATH: GRABBING THE PULASKI AND THE BAMBI BUCKET

A fire burning out of control can be terrifying and deadly. Fighting it takes very strong tools. It also takes strong, brave people. They must have the training and the

Water is just one of the many tools firefighters use to put out wildfires.

courage to walk into an intense blaze and face danger every step of the way.

When you think about tools to fight fires, you may think of large, red fire trucks and long water hoses. In the middle of huge forest fires, however, these tools are not very effective. Instead, firefighters use a variety of other equipment. Some they hold in their hands, while others are huge pieces of machinery.

21ST CENTURY CONTENT

Satellites are helpful in tracking the paths of wildfires, but they can sometimes take hours to transmit photos. Thanks to *Ikhana*, the National Aeronautics and Space Administration's unmanned aircraft, vital data can get to firefighters more quickly. The *Ikhana* is able to photograph fires through the smoke using special sensors. That information is digitally transmitted to fire managers. They use the data to plan their firefighting operations. Other innovations in firefighting technology are miniature weather stations that are mounted on trees. These monitor temperatures and humidity levels. These shoebox-size sensors could help firefighters know where a fire is most likely to start.

Many firefighters head into a fire with 50 to 70 pounds (23 to 32 kilograms) of equipment. This includes gear and protective clothing. One of the first tools that a firefighter uses on the front line is a chainsaw. Firefighters who use them are called sawyers. They cut down trees and create a path for the next team to come through. Sawyers are followed by swampers. These are the people who toss aside the logs, branches, and small trees that have been cut down so that the path is clear. They often use a McLeod, a large rake that can scrape up needles and leaves quickly.

Sometimes a **firebreak** is used to slow down or stop the progress of a wildfire. A firebreak is a natural or constructed gap in materials that add fuel to a fire, such as bushes and shrubs.

Diggers work to make sure there is no fuel in the fire's path.

When the fire reaches the break, it loses its fuel. One of the three parts of the fire triangle fades away, and the fire dies down.

If a firebreak is going to be used, the next people through are the diggers. They use a shovel called a Reinhart and the firefighters' favorite tool, the **Pulaski**. This large axe is perfect for chopping up roots and digging into the ground. For very large firebreaks, bulldozers and tractor plows may be used to move as much dirt as fast as possible.

The teams that usually dig the firebreak are called hand-crews. Once they are finished, it is time for the "hotshots" to come in. These firefighters are the ones who attack the fire and are frequently at the highest risk. They carry a variety of equipment, including fire shelters. They are usually dressed in fire-resistant clothing made from a material called Nomex.

REAL WORLD MATH CHALLENGE

Although in years past, almost all firefighters were men, over the years, more women have joined the profession. How many more firefighters were women in 2008 than in 1983?

Year	Number of Firefighters	Number of Women Firefighters
1983	189,000	1,900
2008	289,400	15,000

(Turn to page 29 for the answer)

Along with these teams, other people are hard at work to help put out wildfires. The fire manager is at headquarters, studying and analyzing every piece of data about the fire. It is his or her job to decide the best way to fight the fire, where to send the firefighters, and what equipment to use. The fire manager usually has a team that helps develop and carry out strategies for putting out the fire. That team also provides firefighters with food and transportation.

Help also comes from the sky in the fight against large wildfires. Helitack crews are firefighters who fly over the flames in helicopters. Smokejumpers can **rappel** down from the hovering helicopters into the site of the fire. These men

Using airplanes and helicopters helps firefighters keep up with fast-moving fires.

and women are frequently the first ones on the scene because they can reach the fire faster than ground crews. Helicopters often carry Bambi buckets. These are filled with hundreds of gallons of water, foam, or other kinds of **retardant**. The copter pilots dump the buckets over parts of the fire and then fly off to have them refilled.

Airplanes known as air tankers also fly over the wildfire and drop water, foam, or retardant. Some of the foam is so sticky that the firefighters call it "sky Jell-O." If the location of the fire is not too remote, large engine crews come to the fire. Their trucks carry 250 to 750 gallons (946 to 2,839 liters) of water and hundreds of feet of hose.

Sometimes, incident meteorologists are dispatched to the scene of a wildfire. These are professionals from the U.S. National Weather Service. They provide critical weather forecasting services, with a special emphasis on tracking wind conditions. Their knowledge of weather conditions, fire behavior, and firefighting make them important members of firefighting teams.

Even after the danger is over and the flames seem to have disappeared, there is work to be done. Firefighters often spend weeks searching through the forest for any smoldering embers or areas showing heat. This process is known as cold trailing. Any time a hot spot is found, firefighters scrape, stir, and soak the spot with water to ensure there is no risk of burning. Additionally, the harsh chemicals in foam and retardants damage the environment. That damage must be repaired so that the forest and its wildlife can recover safely.

CHAPTER FIVE
STOP, DROP, AND ROLL

It is hard to imagine what it would be like to be caught in a wildfire. Do you live near a forest or in an area that gets little rain? Your home might be at risk. Knowing what to do if your home is at risk is important. So is having a fire safety plan in case your home catches on fire. Here are some tips to keep you and your family safe before, during, and after a wildfire:

Wildfires can sometimes spread near towns and cities.

- If you see a wildfire, call 911 immediately. Don't assume someone else has already reported it.
- Get your family and pets out of your house immediately.
- Turn off the natural gas or any other propane or fuel oil supplies.
- If you're trapped inside a house, stay inside. Keep away from outside walls, and close all doors and windows.
- Cover yourself with anything that can shield you from the flames.

REAL WORLD MATH CHALLENGE

Lightning strikes are one of nature's ways of starting a fire. Five U.S. states get the most lightning strikes. The following chart shows the average number of lightning strikes per year during the years 1996 to 2008 in these states. Answer the questions that follow.

Ranking	State	Number of Strikes
1	Texas	2,937,283
2	Florida	1,447,914
3	Oklahoma	1,017,989
4	Missouri	995,744
5	Louisiana	942,128

a. In Texas, how often does lightning strike on average in 1 month? In 1 day?

b. About how much more often does lightning strike in Texas than in Missouri?

(Turn to page 29 for the answers)

LIFE & CAREER SKILLS

Maybe you are fascinated by fire but would rather study it than shoot water or foam at it. If so, perhaps you could become a fire behavior analyst (FBAN). These experts study fire patterns like a detective studies the clues to a crime. They analyze how a fire moves, the shape of the flames, the speed it burns, and the direction it follows. This is typically referred to as the fire's regime. FBANs rely on tools such as high-tech computers and electronic weather kits. They have a strong knowledge of math and science. Using the data gathered by this equipment, analysts provide the firefighters with critical information. They know the type of equipment needed and the number of firefighters necessary to fight the blaze. As one FBAN said during the summer 2011 fires in Florida, "You have to observe what's going on and look for problem areas."

Wildfires have been occurring on our planet since the beginning of time. Thanks to ongoing research, improved technology, and dedicated, trained firefighters, these fires are eventually extinguished. But it's always best to be prepared if you are in a region where wildfire is a risk. Remember these tips, and always be safe and smart about the dangers of fire.

REAL WORLD MATH CHALLENGE ANSWERS

Chapter One

Page 7

A total of 857,329 fires occurred.

92,250 + 84,079 + 73,457 + 63,629 + 65,461 + 66,753 + 96,385 + 85,705 + 78,979 + 78,792 + 71,839 = 857,329 total fires

The most acres were destroyed in 2006.

The fewest were destroyed in 2010.

The difference in acres destroyed between 2006 and 2010 is 6,450,922 acres.

9,873,745 − 3,422,823 = 6,450,922 acres

Chapter Two

Page 13

Equipment failure and burning debris cause fires twice as often as lightning.

3 lightning fires × 2 = 6 fires

Smoking/lighters causes fires half as often as children playing.

22 fires from children playing ÷ 2 = 11 fires

Arson causes four times more fires than smoking/lighters/matches.

11 smoking/lighters/matches fires × 4 = 44 fires

Chapter Three

Page 17

86 new fires began each day.

26,000 total fires ÷ 304 days = 85.53, or 86 fires per day

122 homes were saved each day.

37,000 ÷ 304 days = 121.71, or 122 homes per day

Chapter Four

Page 23

13,100 more women were firefighters in 2008.

15,000 − 1,900 = 13,100 women firefighters

Chapter Five

Page 27

a. Lightning struck 244,774 times per month on average.

2,937,283 ÷ 12 months = 244,773.6 per month

It strikes 8,047 times each day on average.

2,937,283 ÷ 365 days = 8,047.3 per day

b. Lightning strikes three times more often in Texas than in Missouri.

2,987,232 ÷ 995,744 = 3

GLOSSARY

arsonists (AR-suhn-ists) people who deliberately set fire to something

drought (DROUT) a long period of very dry weather

embers (EM-burz) hot, glowing pieces of wood, coal, or other fuel from a fire

extinguish (ek-STING-gwish) to put out a flame, a fire, or a light

firebrands (FIRE-brandz) the embers, or hot, glowing pieces of fuel from a fire

firebreak (FIRE-brake) a gap in materials that add fuel to a fire, such as bushes and shrubs

firestorms (FIRE-stormz) very intense fires that create their own wind system

Pulaski (puhl-AH-skee) a tool used in fighting wildfires; it can be used to dig soil and chop wood

rappel (ruh-PELL) to slide down a rope

retardant (rih-TAR-dent) a chemical used to slow down the progress of a fire

smokejumper (SMOKE-jump-uhr) a firefighter who parachutes into a fire area

tinder (TIN-dur) material that can serve as fuel for a fire

wildfires (WYLD-fiyrz) sweeping, destructive fires occurring in a rural area

FOR MORE INFORMATION

BOOKS

Morrison, Taylor. *Wildfire*. Boston: Houghton Mifflin, 2006.

Silverstein, Alvin, et al. *Wildfires: The Science Behind Raging Infernos*. Berkeley Heights, NJ: Enslow Publishers, 2010.

Sirota, Lyn A. *Out of Control: The Science of Wildfires*. Minneapolis: Compass Point Books, 2009.

WEB SITES

FEMA—Ready Kids
www.ready.gov/kids/index.html
Check out this fun, educational site presented by the U.S. government's Federal Emergency Management Agency (FEMA).

Smokey Bear—Only You Can Prevent Wildfires
www.smokeybear.com/wildfires.asp
Is the part of the United States where you live experiencing a drought? You'll find lots of great information at this site about fire safety, fighting wildfires, and wildfire science. You can also play games that feature colorful animation.

INDEX

ABOUT THE AUTHOR

Tamra Orr is a full-time writer living in the Pacific Northwest. She has written more than 300 books for readers of all ages. She and her husband, four children, dog, and cat moved to Oregon in 2001, so she is familiar with hearing news reports about area wildfires and pays very close attention even though she lives in the city.